HELL

ABIODUN EDUN

CONTENTS

INTRODUCTION

PART ONE

1. Chapter One - Life

2. Chapter Two - Hell

PART TWO

4. Chapter Three - Forgiveness

5. Chapter Four - Thanksgiving

PART THREE

7. Chapter Five - Patience

8. Chapter Six – The Will of God

INTRODUCTION

95% of people on earth do not like challenges. It is wrong to see challenges as problems. When something is a challenge, it means if you look, think, and study very well that situation, you'll surely find a way out. That's why it's a challenge. Challenge is a contest that someone must win either you or the situation facing you. If you allow the situation to defeat you, then you have become a failure and you were not created to be. All that you need to overcome challenges are right inside of you. Only you have to search for them and bring them out.

How can we truly believe God if we don't have challenges bigger than us that will drive us to God in prayer, fasting and studying of His word.

God will remain a distant and mythical spirit that we cannot understand until we experience Him personally in our challenges in the form of hell on earth.

That is why we need to see challenges as God's Avenue for us to experience His faithfulness and power being made manifest in the physical.

God wants to make a name for Himself with your life. But you must be willing to pay the price and believe me, the price is not cheap.

Hell experience will come in different form. Some challenges are so mighty and huge that it takes a man of courage, faith and vision to see God in it.

You may experience hell on earth in marriage, business, health, education and even in your country of residence like Nigeria with the Boko Haram issue.

But know that no matter how bad the situation might be, Jer 29v11 says" I know the thought that I have towards, thought of good and not of evil, to give you a future and a hope". God is never a liar, so hold on to His word; discover yourself to recover your destiny. How do you do that? By being tested of God so that the hidden potentials, gifts, talents and abilities buried inside of you can come to the fore.

Heaven is routing for you and so you cannot allow your earthly hell experience to terminate your destiny.

CHAPTER ONE

Life is a complex and intriguing web of events, occasions and circumstances that every man and woman must go through on this earthly journey.

Situations, events and circumstances can sometimes drive you to the cliff edge of life.

Life is a mountain that everyone must climb. People think it's only the successful few that are climbing mountains. What a wrong belief!! Every man and woman, rich or poor, literate or illiterate has been destined by God to climb mountains in one way or the other.

Having attempted suicide three times myself, but by God's grace and mercy, I was able to overcome that thought and plot of the devil. I discover that everyone climbs to a point on the mountain of life but only few get to the pinnacle of the mountain as destined for them by God.

Those that got tired of climbing almost always make their way to the cliff edge of the mountain and "jump". World famous Canadian singer Michael Bubble said in a track of his song titled 'lost' that life can show no mercy sometimes, it can tear your soul apart, it can make you feel like you've gone crazy but you are not.

Being limited in our ability to see beyond 'now', most humans get tired of going through hell on earth which also means that they get tired of climbing their life mountain to get to the pinnacle of their destiny. For this singular reason, people decide within themselves to 'jump'.

The Bible said that 'if you fail in the days of adversity, which means your strength is small'. Jumping does not necessarily mean committing suicide. Capital 'NO'. Anyone that gets tired of climbing and decided to commit suicide has jumped down the cliff edge of life.

Others got tired and decided to take short cut in getting to the pinnacle. Cutting corners to get to the top simply means you have jumped out of the way and process designed by God for you in getting to the top.

Others got tired and decided to give up the fight. Daddy Adeboye said in the open heavens of one day that we should never give up our hope for a better tomorrow even if today is like you are going through hell on earth.

Some people have agreed with the devil that God did not want them to get to the top of their mountain because of the hell they are going through on earth. For that reason, they decided to jump by letting go of their dreams, aspirations, goals and vision. No wonder the Bible said 'my people perish for lack of vision'.

People that were destined to be MD, CEO and GM of top business conglomerate are now touts at Motor Park, drug addicts and area boys because they couldn't go through hell on earth. They couldn't recognise that 'hard way is the only way' [talking to myself too].

What you did not struggle for will never last in your hand. No wonder the Bible said do everything to stand and having done all, still stand again because no man shall escape experiencing hell on earth one way or another. Some in marriage, some academics, some in business, some in fruitfulness and so on.

Some people might wonder why I am relating hell with life's challenges. The answer is simple. If you study the Bible well, you will see that hell is synonymous with fire. And the Bible said we shall pass through the fire but God will not allow us to get burnt. We can't pass over the fire, around the fire or under the fire but through the fire. The reason is for us to be refined as **GOLD**.

Life's challenges in the form of passing through hell are meant to make us stronger, more flexible and teachable by God, more humble and above all, takes us gradually but steadily to the pinnacle of the mountain of life. World renowned gospel singer Ron Kenoly said 'if you catch hell don't hold it, if you're going through hell don't stop'. He said you go ahead, go ahead, go ahead because God has promised us that His strength is made perfect in our weaknesses.

The song confirms all I said earlier that you must not jump out of the will and purpose of God when life's challenges in the form of hell confront you headlong. All you need to do is ask for grace, strength and humility and tell yourself that you are not jumping.

CHAPTER TWO

There are two types of hell. One is compulsory for all humans but the other is optional. The hell that you pass through on earth is compulsory but the eternal hell reserved for the devil and his cohorts is optional.

How you performed in passing through your earthly hell will almost always determine whether you go to eternal hell or not. The beggar called Lazarus in the Bible endured hell on earth but was carried to Abraham's bosom after death.

Ron Kenoly said if you catch hell don't hold it and if you're going through hell don't stop. You just go ahead, go ahead and go ahead. Many people have decided to jump at the cliff edge of their mountain into cultism in school because it comes with temporary benefits which includes power to torment lecturers and student alike, raping students at will and subtle way of stealing from fellow students who can't defend themselves.

Some have gone into secret society in order to cut short their hell experiences manifesting in the form of poverty and barrenness. Even some of God's servants have jumped because of delay in crowd explosion in their ministry and have gotten power from demons and idols.

Though these people double cross their earthly hell surely by their actions, but they are sure candidate for president, senators, governors and commissioners in eternal hell.

God arranged for you to go through hell on earth so that you can even see the stuff those around us are made of. Meaning like when things are sweet and rosy, people tend to flock around you and you wouldn't know your enemies from friends but when you are facing hell on earth, when life's challenges are biting you really hard then you'll see how people treat you.

Some people in their time of needs have been deserted by even the closest of family, relatives and friends. Wife leave husband in time of need and great challenges i.e. she jumps and even men do same too. God also allow you experience hell on earth in order to confirm His word which says 'woe unto him that makes an arm of flesh his defence'. Why because God is the only one that cannot fail but human being will run from you at the slightest change in fortune.

Like the marriage vow which says for better for worse, for richer or poorer and so on. Now in our time, it is for better for stay, for worse for to run. People are now looking for where the grass is greener because nobody wants to suffer forgetting that in life, you have two options; to live long and see evil or don't see evil but die young.

John 16v33 surely comes to mind when talking about Christian and non-Christian experiencing hell on earth. Jesus Christ said that our peace is in Him because in this world, you will go through hell in the form of hunger, tribulation, affliction, sickness and persecution. But He said you should rejoice because you will surely have the victory at the end. But many at times you get so battered by these challenges that you ask if God really exist. Indeed, He does exist and He's observing every action and steps of faith you take in your hell challenges on earth. No wonder you discover that God chooses what you go through but you must choose how you go through your hell experience on earth.

Hell, experience on earth is meant to make you better, not bitter. The adage in Yoruba says 'the afflicter is only trying to make you stronger' (adani l'oro fi agbara k'oni).

If a man can make up his mind that there's nothing, he cannot endure certainly his fears will leave him.

CHAPTER THREE

I want to tell the story of a young man who left Nigeria for the United Kingdom some years ago. He had so many challenges while in Nigeria to the extent that after graduation, he couldn't get a job for years. He had a very good result but still couldn't get a job.

Eventually after many fasting and praying, deliverance service and confession of sin, God opened the door to the UK How joyful this young man was and he made a promise to make something of his life. He thought pounds is something you get on the road or side street but alas, he was wrong. He laboured so much to the best of his abilities and was living an average life in the UK.

He had no resident permit and this kind of made it difficult for him to do any decent job. He only managed to get a job through a good friend and his family. He enrolled in school, paid so much money and persisted in every hell experience that came his way. He was attacked, ridiculed, mocked and rejected by friends, neighbours and even family members in the UK but he continues to endure.

He went through hell in terms of relationship experiencing so much disappointment and heartbreak but he persisted and endured everything. He finished the school programme, wrote a book which he sent to the US and is still in the process of being printed and at last, got married in the winter of 2009.

He thought after marriage that he and his wife will file for permit to live in the UK and start to live the lives of their dreams. He had 'great expectation' (the title of one of Charles Dickens novel) but his dreams and aspirations got shattered not even up to a year into marriage.

Unknown to him, one of his friends had secretly phoned the police to reveal his status and that of his wife. In his mind, the end to his hell experience was in sight. He thought with the school degree and years of stay in the UK that he stood a better chance of getting a job that will settle him and bring about peace and fulfilment. But suddenly the police came, arrested him and his wife and put them in prison. He never slept in a prison before up till that point and that one night sleep in the cell was enough hell experience to make him jump from the cliff edge of his mountain but he thought of his wife.

They were moved to a removal centre where they fought the removal order issued against them. They fought with their little savings coupled with great support from some family members and friends.

I ask myself why the friend betrayed him and the answer I got was jealousy and envy because to the glory of God, his wedding was one of the talks of the town in south east London in 2009 and the friend couldn't think of any other thing but to hand him over to the authority like Judas did to Jesus Christ.

Now let's pause here. When Jesus was betrayed and was been nailed to the cross, he prayed for forgiveness for those soldiers nailing him. Why? Because of the love he had for us humans. If you say you love someone and have never suffered for that person to the extent that you cry and get humiliated, honestly ask yourself if indeed you love that person.

Daniel Beddingfield said 'nothing hurts like 'LOVE' and nothing gives your heart so much pain like 'LOVE'. Many people have committed suicide because they were dumped by either boyfriend or girlfriend; many have gone into drugs because they couldn't cope with the betrayal by close business associate or family members. The list is just endless but in all, we have to do what Jesus did, FORGIVE.

This young man is now in Nigeria fighting to start his life all over but the hell he's now experiencing all over has opened his eyes to see that only God can be trusted 100%.

Let's quickly look at another story. You can say the friend of that young man was not a Christian and that was why he betrayed him. Was Judas not a believer? Why did he betray Jesus then?

The story was told of a pastor who was doing well in ministry and family. One day, the elders of the church came and asked why he defrauded the church to the tune of millions of naira. He vehemently denied the allegation and subsequently was arrested by the police. He sorts for support from people but no one believed him even the wife and children too.

He was charged to court and sentenced to about six years in prison. The humiliation and disgrace the man suffered was enough for him to jump from the way of light which he received the day he accepted Jesus.

He prayed and fasted that the truth be revealed before all he laboured for will go down the drain but God did nothing. Why? Because the time has come for him to have his hell experience on earth. What he had been preaching.i.e. forgiveness is now what God wanted to use as a test for him.

Some years later, a man approached the elders of the church because he was also experiencing hell in his life.

His family was disintegrating. He had no peace, sickness was in his life and his business was crumbling.

The man in question used to be the accountant of the pastor in prison. This man who was a believer took this bold step to approach the elders of the church because he was the real culprit and not the pastor.

He was the one that forged the pastor's signature, collected millions of naira and resigned to go start a business.

Even though God did not reveal the truth at the beginning, He still turned around to torture the former accountant having seen the hell experience the man of God was going through in prison. The pastor was at that point dejected and alone because the wife and children have left and promised never to return. They couldn't forgive him for what they believed he did.

After the confession of the former accountant, the elders promptly consulted the church lawyer who called in the police and arrested the man. He gave a written confession which was used to file an appeal on behalf of the pastor so as to secure his release.

When the elders came to him to give him the news that they thought was good to him, he busted into tears and said there and then that he will never forgive that former accountant until they both get to heaven.

Now can you blame the young man in the first story if he refuses to forgive like the pastor? Many people especially Christians or believers think it's an easy thing to forgive. If someone hurts you really deeply, I'll want to believe that the first thing that will come to your mind will be revenge or retaliation. I've been there and I'm still there. On so many occasions I've had to battle thoughts of revenge, retaliation and even malice. Devil makes sure he reminds you per second how much pain you've been caused and why you just cannot let it pass.

Even if you manage to forgive, it takes time to forget because the devil plays the event over and over in your mind. If not for the grace of God then the whole world would have turned upside down when it gets to the issue of forgiveness.

Let's look at Nigeria for instance. People think because the Bible said you should forgive now means some group can start killing believer at will. That is not good. We should stop hurting ourselves intentionally and deliberately.

At any rate, the Bible implores you to forgive anyone who sinned against you. The Bible said forgive so that your heavenly father can forgive you your sins too.

This young man in the story often wondered why God will want him to forgive someone who destroyed all he had ever laboured for in life.

The answer is not far-fetched because the Bible said 'all things worketh together for GOOD to them that love God and are called according to His purposes and plans. The ways of God are not your ways and sometimes He allows things to happen that you don't understand why.

If God allows the devil working through a friend or family member to do you evil, sincerely pray for the grace to forgive and forget so you can learn what He wants you to learn and move on in life. God does nothing without a reason.

Can you blame the pastor too? No but he needs to ask for grace to forgive and forget so he can move on. Many of us are going through hell because we refuse to let go of those who had done us evil. You can understand why some wives do not want to see their in-laws simply because they were tormented during their years of barrenness.

No matter your hell experience on earth, know that God designed every hell experience you go through or you are going through for His glory to be revealed in your life and situation. What did Abraham do wrong that made God sent his descendants to Egypt to be enslaved for 430yrs?

Some people experience their hell in the hands of business associate that duped them and render them penniless. Some were maltreated, abused and molested by their husband. All these are hell experiences that we must go through on earth but in all, we must be ready to forgive and forget and move on.

Forgiveness is a very tough decision to make in all honesty but have you ever seen a car carrying a load meant for a 50-tonne truck? No way. If it does, it will never be able to move. Unforgiveness is like carrying excess baggage on our journey of life. The journey is tough as it is why add excess baggage of unwanted burdens to it.

You have a mountain to climb. The top is your priority but if you allow excess and unnecessary baggage, it will definitely slow you down and may even prevent you from ever making it to the top of your mountain. Let go and let God.

My brother Adewale Adedigba, the author of 'living a successful life' said you must understand your environment for you to succeed in that environment. Now what makes up the environment? Climate, land, water and other natural and man-made things that we can see. But the most important factor in an environment is 'man'.

It thus means that you need to understand that man will offend you, put you through hell on this earth in order for you to get to your promised land and fulfil destiny.

Study the life of Joseph in Genesis. For him to fulfil his destiny, God had to use his own blood brothers to take him through hell experience on earth.

Many of us are complacent and non challant that without something biting us in the bum, we will not move.

The worst atrocity that can be committed against a man is for his own family to sell him into slavery like Joseph. Many of us are going through hell today because of some devilish people around us who are actually instrument in the hand of God in taking us to our destination.

Brethren, in order not to prolong our hell experience, let's ask God for grace and determine that unforgiveness will not elongate our hell experience on earth.

Parents forgive your children and children too forgive your parents. Let's forgive our leaders whether in the church, nation, company and family and let leaders also forgive their followers too.

In doing this and by God's grace and mercy, we can be guaranteed that our hell experience on earth will not be prolonged more than necessary.

Job said 'though He slays me, yet will I praise Him'. Even though God take us through hell on earth, if we forgive and endure, definitely we'll have a glorious story to tell in the end.

A man who doesn't want to go through hell on earth is dead because as long as we live, we'll always experience challenges testing our faith to show whether we are still in God or not?

Are you on God's side still?

CHAPTER FOUR

Someone with a heart of gratitude can be likened to someone with a heart of gold.

Gold is precious and everybody both young and old do always like to have gold jewelleries or ornaments. A man with a heart of gratitude always attracts great blessings, favour and honour from God and humans alike. No wonder Yoruba people said 'someone who received a good gesture but could not say thank you is worse than an armed robber'. One of the things that could make a man experience hell on earth beyond imagination is to be ungrateful to God and man. The Bible said 'give thanks in every situation because that is the will of God for you in Christ Jesus'.

Most of the time, we find it difficult or really hard to say thank you especially to God because of what we are expecting from Him. But we forget that it's because He gave us life in the first place that we can hope for something at all. If God asked for our soul right now, who will stand against God to ask Him why?

Why do we need to thank God at all? Because the Bible said God will not test us more than we can bear but even in the hell experience will also make a way of escape. It is better to say thank you God no matter the situation. Take for instance the story of the ten lepers in the Bible who came to Jesus for healing. After receiving their miracle, only one came back to say thank you and for that heart of gratitude, he made his healing permanent and everlasting.

No matter the pain, agony, sorrow, hunger, sickness, tribulation, affliction, depression, discouragement, disappointment and failure that you may experience in life, you should always remember to say thank you God because it could have been worse.

Your hell experience should not make you ungrateful in any way. Paul asked what can separate us from the love of God. He answered by saying nothing because no matter what you are passing through, your life is in God's hands.

Let's see something about that young man in the earlier chapter. Even though things were tough and challenging in the UK but still, God was making a way somehow but, this young man has one terrible attitude, he was ungrateful to God.

All he does was to complain, grumble and at one time even called God 'WICKED'.

You must be careful of what comes out of your mouth when going through your hell experience (s) on earth.

Even after marriage, God provided for him a job that brings in steady income but still, he couldn't find reasons to thank God. His wife advised him to always thank God which he does out of compulsion once a while. Know one thing that such thank you is not acceptable to God. Thanking God in difficult situation has no good to do for God but it's for your own benefit because a grateful heart is a joyful heart and when you have the joy of the Lord in your heart, even the greatest of mountain becomes easy for you to surmount.

You may be in similar situation today like that young man. Maybe your mates are in chevron, shell, zenith bank and other high paying salary job while you are just managing in a primary school as a teacher. Your mates' lives in duplexes and luxurious flats in choice areas, drives expensive jeep and cars while your two legs are your treasured means of transport which has worn out your shoes due to the trekking and you find it difficult to see why you should thank God. To tell you the truth, the hell experience and dryness you're going through right now will be nothing compared to what you'll experience should God decide to show you how much He detest people who cannot say thank you.

Please learn a hard lesson from this young man. He continued to complain forgetting the day a man came spiritually to attack him and if not for God's mercy, he would have been dead by now. He forgot the day pepper spray was sprayed into his eyes too but for God's mercy, he would by now have become a one-eyed man. What about the day he got knocked down by a car still in the UK and didn't have a scratch on his body? He forgot all these benefits of God in times past and Bible said in psalms 'praise the Lord oh my soul and forget not all His benefits'.

He was always complaining because his demands have not been met by God. He thought he was experiencing hell on earth then but now, after landing in Nigeria couple of years back and without any source of income, no money and begging to survive, this young man has now come to appreciate God for what he had then but which he didn't cherish and God took away.

He learnt what it means to say thank you the hard way. Assuming he had cultivated the habit of thanking God then maybe God could have averted the trap set for him by the friend and household enemies.

But to know that God loves him when he thought he was hated by God, God had to allow him go through hell now so as to know the difference. How he wishes God can restore him back to his old estate now.

The Bible said the 'joy' of the Lord is our strength but a man who cannot say thank you can never experience that joy. Count your blessings; name them one by one and it will surprise you what the Lord has done.

A man with a heart of gratitude sees God in every hell experience he or she is going through. Because of this, God automatically averts many dangers and evil for a man with a heart of gratitude. He removes evil, frustration and attack from that man or woman even when it's like all hope is lost. Always find reason(s) to thank God even in that hell experience you're going through. You may not see it now but sooner or later, the siege against your life will give way as a result of your thanksgiving.

Try it and see that it works like magic. Don't learn the hard way like that young man. Don't compete with anyone but maintain your peace and thank Him and surely, He will intervene for you in a way that will amaze you.

Please try it today.

Cultivate the heart of gratitude otherwise the devil will tempt you to jump from the cliff edge of your mountain. The mountain top is your focus and goal and one of the ways to get there is by having a heart of gratitude.

Many have jumped off their mountain by committing suicide because they can't find enough reason(s) to thank God in their lives, family and business. Many have yielded their hearts to jump into alternatives that will prolong their hell experience on earth. Though there will be a fake sense of achievement and fulfilments for now but remember, the devil does not give any lasting joy. Whatever you have collected from the devil now, be sure to know that you'll pay back for it twenty-fold in years to come in tears and sorrow.

So be careful to observe your life and always find reasons to thank God and be joyful. By that you'll be able to endure whatever hell experience you are going through right now and sooner than later, the morning of your joy will dawn. Focus on God and be grateful always and you shall get to the pinnacle of your destiny in Jesus' name.

CHAPTER FIVE

I long to scale the utmost height,

Though rough the way,

And hard the fight,

My song while climbing shall resound,

Lord lead me on to higher ground.

(This song is taken from the Redeem Hymn Book)

To scale the utmost height in life with the road rough and hard, you need one very great virtue which is 'patience'. Slow and steady wins the race is a popular saying. Patience is another trait that can help you to endure and bear any hell experience (s) that you are passing through right now on earth.

A man of patience like Job is sure to get to the top of his mountain. Job waited patiently for God to restore him while going through hell on earth.

One of the things that can make you jump from the cliff edge of your mountain is lack of patience. Many people including

Christians alike have been infected with what is called the 'NOW SYNDROME'. We want something and we want it now irrespective of the danger that blessing poses to our lives and that of people around us.

God said to Paul my grace is sufficient for you. Meaning that you have to exercise patience whenever you are in a difficult situation. Yes, no food to eat be patient. No job, yes be patient. No child in your marriage yet (especially for men and husband family), be patient. In everything that you are passing through in life, God expect you to be patient and have long suffering.

The story was told of a man who was poor and in need of breakthrough. So, he went to God and asked that God remove the poverty far from him. God said okay and promised to help.

Not long after that, God came with four multiple choices; money, children, long life and patience for him to choose one.

This made the man even more confused than before. He went to his wives and asked for their opinions.

The first wife said children. Why he asked? Because children are the heritage of the Lord and blessed is the man who had his quivers full of them and above all, it is the person that has children that is prosperous in life.

He turned to the second wife but she said money. Why? Because money answers all things and it's the wheel of the gospel. And to crown it all, we'll be able to afford whatever we want in life, she concluded.

Because he wasn't pleased with their answers, he decided to consult his parents for elderly advice.

He narrated his problem and his parents said to him to choose patience. He got infuriated at the mention of this because that was the last thing he wanted to hear. How can he be patient when he was suffering and going through hell?

He went back home sad than he was earlier. He pondered on the words of his parents and decided eventually to follow their advice. Yoruba adage says 'the words of elders are words of wisdom'.

He went back to God and chooses 'patience'. After a while, children said he couldn't stay without patience and so God released children to go and live with patience and same goes for the other two; money and long life.

Before long, this man became rich, fruitful and blessed with long life all because he decided to choose patience. He reaped the reward of being patient in the end.

Many of us are going through hell in the form of challenges. Our parents have told us to be patient but we refused. Our pastors have told us to exercise patience but we called their bluff.

We want money now, children now, expensive cars and big mansions now and luxurious holidays to Asia, Europe, America and the Caribbean nations. The Bible said 'seek ye first the kingdom of God and His righteousness and all the other things shall be added unto you'. Bible also said counts it all joy when you're going through challenges because everything works out to build up your person and make you more patient.

My people, patience pays. If that man had jumped or had not taken patience but let's say had taken money, it's possible that it's that money that will lead to his destruction and downfall.

Having a hell experience is like waiting for what you have planted to germinate, grow and bear fruit. God uses the hell experience you go through to teach you a lesson about life and test whether you will appreciate those things you are looking unto Him for. No wonder the Yoruba adage says 'what you do not suffer for will never last in your hands'. God wants you to cherish His blessings and provisions. He wants you to see that it's not your power that has gotten you the wealth, peace, joy and prosperity that you enjoy but His mercies.

Gold must pass through fire before its beauty can show. So also, you as Christians and people in general must be prepared to face challenges. God knows the correct fire temperature to allow you pass through and if you know God can never make mistake, then you just have to be patient with Him and let Him do a fantastic job with your life. Otherwise, your hell experience may be prolonged more than necessary.

Let me tell you another story to buttress the importance of patience.

A married woman noticed that the love between her and her husband had diminished. She consulted an herbalist who told her to go get the breast milk of a nursing lioness for a love charm.

She spoke with powerful hunters on how they can help her get the milk from the lioness. To her amazement, all of them declined. Their reasons was that a lioness is dangerous but a nursing one is suicide.

Determined to get what she wanted, this woman asked for where she can get a nursing lioness and she was given the location by a hunter who came across one.

She went and bought a whole cow, cut it into small chunks which she roasted and carried into the jungle in the direction of the nursing lioness.

She hid herself far away on a tree and from there started throwing the lioness chunks of meat. She did this for some days and eventually showed herself to the lioness from a distance. She threw couple of meat to the lioness and went away making sure that the lioness saw her.

She did this for some few days and after that started approaching the animal little by little with meat in her hands. She finally got close that she was able to touch the lioness. She would come around every day and play with the lioness. Each time as usual, she brought meat which means the lioness does not have to labour for food. Little by little she started to play with the animal, rubbing her hairy body all over.

The first time she tried to take milk from the animal, she growled at her and she backed off. But she persisted and each time the animal growled at her, she'll quickly drop meat for her. Eventually, the animal allowed her to play with her and even allowed her take some milk into a container she brought with her. What great and mighty hunters could not do has been done by an ordinary woman.

She was overjoyed when she got back to the herbalist with the precious commodity in her hand. The old man could not believe it and after narrating how she got it, the man had nothing but admiration for her and saluted her resilience, patience and courage.

She asked the old man when to come back for the love portion. To her greatest shock, the man said she doesn't need to come back and that the love charm is already in her hands. She asked the old man the meaning of his statement. The old man cleared his throat and said 'my daughter, there is no love portion that I can do for you. If you can make a nursing lioness love you to the extent of parting with her precious milk, then I can't see why you need a love portion to win back your husband's love.

My advice, the man continued is to go back to your husband and use the same strategy of patience and resilience you used on that lioness, and I'm sure you'll have you husband's love back.

'Only the patient can milk a lioness'. Your husband is not as dangerous as that lioness and I'm sure if you adopt the same strategy, all will be well. Our elders say 'the patient can cook stones soft'.

Tell me now, does patience pay or not? Make your judgement.

The woman went through hell to get the milk but with patience and she came out unscathed.

Patience is a virtue you cannot do without if you want to fulfil your destiny in life.

CHAPTER SIX

The will of God simply put means the purpose and plan of God for all His children. Even those who have sold their hearts and will to the devil were originally a part of God's plan because there's no man on earth who was born without God having a purpose and plan for that individual.

There is nothing like accidental birth in God's divine order. God has no bastard among his creature. The term bastard came from us humans. Illegitimate, OSU (slave) and other derogatory names used to qualify fellow human being were not God's idea at creation.

If you fall into these categories like OSU (slave), bastard and illegitimate and these names are making your life hell, rejoice today because even though people gave you no chance, and you can say life has been hell and difficult, know that God wants to show forth his glory through you. Only discover His purpose and will for your life and you will definitely rule your world.

Not knowing the will of God can make a man experience hell on earth. If you know the plan and purpose of God for your life, I say congratulation but that is just phase 1.

Knowing the will of God for your life and fulfilling it are two different things entirely. But if you do not know the will of God for your life, then you have a gigantic task ahead of you in this life.

What were you created for by God?

If you search the Bible, you will see people who recognised the will of God for their lives early and grabbed the opportunity with both hands. But sadly, some characters in the same Bible also knows the plan and purpose of God for their lives but couldn't actualise it.

Our Lord Jesus Christ from his early age recognises the plan and purpose of God for His life. Even when he was growing up and working as a carpenter, he never lost focus of what God sent him to earth to do.

Our Lord Jesus Christ experienced so much hardship on earth. Before his ministry finally kicked off, he had to be baptized and led onto the wilderness for forty days and nights fasting and praying. No wonder the devil came to tempt him because the devil thought he would be vulnerable at that point. Yes, he was vulnerable in the flesh but very much alive in the spirit and was able to beat the devil hands down. How many times did Jesus' sleep without food? He had no house of his own not to talk of getting married.

Why? Because he knows that all these things like home, wife and children will hinder him from fulfilling the plan and purpose of God for his life. The will of God was for him to die and reconcile man back to God. He discovered it (the plan and purpose of God}, and passionately pursued it.

Even in the garden, he confirmed that the will of God was for him to die that horrible death on the cross and shed his blood as ransom for us so we can cross from hell into heaven. To fulfil this certainly was hell for him. He was beaten, battered and bruised all that the will of God for us humans can be actualized.

And examine his life. He sure finished the race set before him in a blaze of glory and honour with God having given him a name above every other name both in heaven and on earth.

Paul discovered the will and purpose of God for his life on the road to Damascus. Not giving it a second thought, he wholeheartedly embraced the plan and purpose of God for his life and in the process became the greatest apostle ever. What about Samuel and other men of God in the Bible who went through hell, humiliation and shame to fulfil the plan and purpose of God for their lives.

A pastor was asked to walk naked in Israel because God wanted to tell the Israelites something. He didn't object because he had already accepted the call of God upon his life. The will of God made him walk naked.

I don't think any man of God in this era can ever agree to walk naked as part of the will of God for his or her life. Another man of God married a prostitute. Having known the plan and purpose of God for his life, he had no option but to marry the prostitute as directed by God.

Sadly, some people discovered the plan and purpose of God for their lives but still miss it at the end.

One that readily jumps to mind is Samson. A nazarite from birth. An ordained judge from the womb but he allowed lust to destroy his life. He started very well but ended badly.

To be able to endure any hell experience you are going through right now on earth, you must understand the will of God for your life. No man can ever be truly happy until he had discovered the purpose and plan of God for his life. A man without a purpose is a man living an 'aimless life'. Knowing the will of God for your life makes it possible for you to set goals and targets that will help you in fulfilling that purpose of God for your life.

We must careful though to point out one thing. Even though the Bible said we should give thanks no matter the situation because it is the will of God for us in Christ Jesus. But it is not all hell experience (s) on earth that is the will of God for our lives. The devil secretly punishes us sometimes under the guise that it's the will of God. For this we've got to be able to pray and fast, study the word and find out genuinely what the will of God is in that situation.

It is not all hell experiences on earth that will lead you to the discovery of your purpose neither is all hell experiences a means to us fulfilling our purpose too. We have to pray, fast, study the word and search our lives carefully and God in His mercies will surely reveal our purpose on earth.

Even in secular life, we must consciously labour to discover our purpose. Are you created to be an employer of labour? If you don't discover the purpose and plan of God for your life, you'll only be labouring for nothing. Are you destined to be a lecturer but you are now working as a banker? Sorry, all you will experience will be frustration and disappointment.

Bill Gates discovered his purpose in life and founded Microsoft, sir Richard Branson started Virgin, sir Philip Green founded Bhs, Steve Jobs co-founder apple inc, Henry Ford founded the Ford Motor company. The list is just endless.

People that discover the purpose and plan of God for their lives will definitely leave behind a mark that can never be erased in history.

Even in politics, you can fulfil the plan and purpose of God for your life like Abraham Lincoln of the USA and Winston Churchill of Great Britain and so on.

Even in Nigeria, we had great politicians and statesmen that discovered their purposes and followed it with their whole heart, strength and blood.

Like chief Obafemi Awolowo, Dr Azikwe, Dr Enahoro to mention a few.

Even in your generation today, we are privileged to have men of God who discovered the plan and purpose of God for their lives and they pursued it vigorously. Daddy Adeboye and Papa Oyedepo are world known men of God who gave up everything to discover the plan and purpose of God for their lives. Today, you know the story of their lives.

To discover the will of God for your life will not come easy. If you get it on a platter of gold, you will not cherish it. You need to pray, fast and study the word of God for you to discover your purpose in life. For those in the secular world, whatever you find yourself doing easily without any struggle and you can do better than others may probably be the purpose of God for your life.

Even when you discover your purpose, the devil will not want you to fulfil it. He lost out on the purpose of God for his life and is not happy seeing anyone fulfilling God ordained plans and purposes.

When you are going through hell on earth, please examine yourself. It might be a way of God calling you into your destiny. Sometimes we are forced to cry out to God when it's like we cannot bear the pain we are going through any longer. And in situations like that, God do reveal to us his plans and purposes for our lives.

Moses wanted to see the great sight of the burning bush which was not consumed. In turning to look, God arrested him and he discovered his purpose in life. The will of God came to bear on this wanted murderer.

Not discovering the purpose and plan of God for your life will definitely bring discouragement and dejection as we climb the mountain of life. Many people will jump off the cliff edge of their mountain because they do not know what the will of God is in that situation.

Discover the will of God for your life and fulfil your destiny. Lastly, one key factor that comes with accepting the will of God is 'faith'. It's only a man of faith that will ever believe God's prompting when going through a terrible situation. Faith is crucial in knowing the will of God. Even if God reveal His will for your life, you need faith to agree with Him because you know God is the Alpha and Omega.

Let's look at Daddy Adeboye who was a professor of applied mathematics at the University of Lagos then. When God called him into his destiny as a pastor, he didn't oppose the plan of God for his life. Why? The answer is because he had faith in a God that can never make mistake and we can see how the whole story pans out today.

Without faith it is impossible to please God and so in searching for the will of God for our individual lives, we must have faith knowing fully well that that plan and purpose of God may take us far away from our comfort zone and easy life. But because we want to impact our generation for good, we must be humble enough to submit to God and follow whatever path He has ordained for us in life and be sure, the top is our limit.

CONCLUSION

Our attitude determines our altitude.

Your disposition to the various life's challenges that you face will determine whether you will get out of that problem or not. Wait upon the Lord and renew your strength and I assure you that every life's challenges in the form of hell will surely give way like the red sea.

Nothing can stop you from getting to the top but you can stop yourself.

Man's greatest enemy is himself. Conquer this enemy and surely, you are on your way to fulfilling your destiny.

God bless you all.

www.ingramcontent.com/pod-product-compliance
Lightning Source LLC
Chambersburg PA
CBHW070940220526
45469CB00007B/2461